Whispers of the Eternal

Shyamankar Singhari

WHISPERS OF THE ETERNAL

First Edition, 2025

Published by WKRISHIND

ISBN: 978-81-992468-9-8

For the dreamers who hear the whispers of the stars, and the seekers who chase the light within their hearts.

I am large, I contain multitudes. —Walt Whitman, "Song of Myself" (1892)

ACKNOWLEDGMENTS

To my family and friends, whose unwavering support lit the path for these words. To the poets and dreamers who came before, your whispers inspired my own. And to the universe, for its endless stories that echo in every heart.

YOUR HEART

Your heart creates hate inside you,
Which sparks love within me.
My love, my smile,
The energy born from your hate
Gives me strength to survive this world.

The day after, the sun will rise high,
You'll soar like a fly.
You shun the light of the sun,
Yet crave its gentle glow.
Don't be upset—
One day your flower will bloom bright,
You'll stand proud,
Your blossoms will rise,
Your head held high.
This day is yours—
Powerful, strong, and wise.

Dream Girl

One day a sweet girl
Will meet me.
She will dream for me,
Gift me a sweet dream.
She will be no mere girl—
A pearl, radiant and round.
Together we'll blend,
A compound, forever bound.

How Am I?

Images flicker in my mind,
Turning into words.
My mind signals my thumbs,
My thumbs weave these words.
My words whisper—I'm breathing,
My breaths pulse—I'm alive.
My pulse sings—I'm here.

My heart, my smile,
This is my answer to your question—
How am I?

SOMETHING NEW

I yearn to do something new,
To shine like stars above.
Stars hold light, light holds energy,
Energy sparks fire—I crave to inspire.
I seek not to be a lover,
But to grow more human.
I shed the weight of poverty,
Embracing true humanity.
Oh, I've found humanity!
Oh, I've found poverty's light!
Yes, I shine like a star—
I've won my war.
Now, I blaze like a star!

WHY?

Asking "Why?"
The things that happened,
"Loving" was my try.
I'm not a bad guy.
Hey, Universe! I'm your sky.
Let my eyes not be criminal,
I'm you, and you are mine.
Asking "Why?"
Do you wish me to cry?
My loving Universe,
Asking "Why?"
Am I a bad guy?

SILENT ECHOES

In the quiet of my soul's deep night,
A whisper hums, a fleeting light.
Echoes of dreams that never fade,
Soft as moonlight, sharp as a blade.

My heart hums low, a secret song,
Of paths I've walked, both right and wrong.
Each step a note, each breath a rhyme,
Carving my truth through endless time.

Do you hear it, too, in the still air?
The echo of hopes we used to share?
They linger, soft, in the heart's embrace,
Guiding my steps to a sacred place.

Chasing Shadows

I chase the shadows across the dawn,
Fleeting forms that are here, then gone.
They dance in the light, they slip through my hands,
Like grains of time, like desert sands.

Each shadow holds a piece of me,
A fleeting truth I long to see.
In their darkness, I seek the light,
A spark to guide me through the night.

Run, I will, till my feet grow sore,
Chasing dreams I can't ignore.
For in the shadows, I find my call,
To rise, to love, to conquer all.

STARLIT PATH

Beneath the stars, I walk alone,
On paths of light, on trails of stone.
Each twinkling beam a story told,
Of hearts once warm, now grown cold.

Yet in their glow, I find my way,
Through endless night to breaking day.
The stars above, they call my name,
Ignite my soul with cosmic flame.

No fear can bind, no doubt can sway,
My steps align with light's soft play.
The starlit path, my heart's true guide,
Leads me where dreams and truth collide.

WHISPERS OF DAWN

The dawn breaks soft, a tender sigh,
Painting whispers across the sky.
Each hue a promise, each ray a vow,
To live, to love, to be here now.

I stand in silence, heart awake,
Feeling the world begin to shake.
The morning hums, a gentle plea,
To find the self I'm meant to be.

RIVER'S LULLABY

The river sings a lullaby,
Its waters dance beneath the sky.
Each ripple tells of ancient streams,
Carrying hopes, reflecting dreams.

I dip my hands, I feel its grace,
A fleeting touch, a warm embrace.
The river knows my heart's deep cry,
And sings me soft, its lullaby.

FADING LIGHT

The light retreats, the day grows dim,
Yet hope still burns within my hymn.
Each fading ray, a soft goodbye,
Leaves stars to bloom in night's wide sky.

I hold the dusk, I greet the dark,
Each shadow hides a waiting spark.
Though light may fade, my soul takes flight,
To chase the glow beyond the night.

Wings of Dust

On wings of dust, my spirit flies,
Through endless voids and starlit skies.
Each grain a tale of time's long reign,
Of joy, of loss, of love, of pain.

I soar where winds and dreams entwine,
Where heart and cosmos both align.
These wings of dust, though frail they seem,
Carry my soul to every dream.

Beneath the Veil

Beneath the veil of twilight's glow,
Secrets whisper, soft and low.
The world unveils its hidden face,
A truth that time cannot erase.

I walk where shadows gently fall,
Hearing the night's eternal call.
Beneath the veil, I come alive,
Where heart and mystery both thrive.

Echoes of You

Your voice still lingers in the air,
A fleeting echo, everywhere.
Each word a thread that binds my heart,
Though time and space now keep us apart.

I trace your name in starlit skies,
See your reflection in my eyes.
The echoes hum, they never fade,
A love eternal, softly made.

WOVEN DREAMS

My dreams are woven, thread by thread,
Of hopes I've held, of words I've said.
Each strand a wish, each knot a prayer,
Spun in the heart's unyielding air.

The loom of life keeps spinning still,
Guided by fate, by choice, by will.
These woven dreams, they light my way,
From dusk's embrace to breaking day.

TIDES OF TIME

The tides of time roll soft and slow,
Through valleys deep where memories grow.
Each wave a story, carved in stone,
Of hearts once joined, now left alone.

I stand upon the shore of years,
Washing my soul with silent tears.
Yet in the tides, I find my place,
A timeless heart, a boundless grace.

Silent Flame

A silent flame burns deep within,
Where shadows end and hopes begin.
It flickers soft, yet holds its ground,
A quiet strength, a sacred sound.

No storm can dim its steady glow,
No doubt can halt its endless flow.
This flame, my soul, will ever burn,
Till stars to dust and skies return.

HORIZON'S CALL

The horizon calls with whispered light,
A beacon blazing through the night.
Each step I take, it draws me near,
Dissolving doubt, dissolving fear.

I run to meet its boundless edge,
To leap from earth, to take the pledge.
The horizon's song, my heart's own beat,
Where sky and soul forever meet.

Embers of Hope

Embers of hope glow soft and red,
In ashes of dreams long thought dead.
Each spark a chance to rise anew,
To paint the world in vibrant hue.

I fan the flames with every breath,
Defying sorrow, defying death.
These embers hold my heart's true scope,
A fire eternal, born of hope.

Moonlit Vow

Beneath the moon, I make my vow,
To live, to love, to be here now.
Its silver light, my solemn guide,
Reveals the truth I hold inside.

No chain can bind, no fear can stay,
My heart's resolve in moonlight's play.
This vow I keep, through joy and pain,
Till moon and stars return again.

BREATH OF EARTH

The earth exhales, a gentle sigh,
Its breath a song beneath the sky.
Each blade of grass, each ancient tree,
Whispers its truth, its mystery.

I breathe with earth, our pulses blend,
A bond no time can ever end.
In every gust, I hear its call,
To rise, to live, to give my all.

FLICKER OF TRUTH

A flicker of truth in darkness gleams,
A spark that lights my deepest dreams.
It dances soft, yet burns so bright,
A guide through doubt, a beacon's light.

I hold it close, this fleeting flame,
It knows my heart, it knows my name.
In truth's small spark, I find my way,
From shadowed night to endless day.

Wanderer's Song

I sing the song of wanderers free,
Whose hearts are bound to destiny.
Through fields and stars, through storm and calm,
I carry hope, a soothing balm.

Each note I sing, a step I take,
A path where dreams and fates awake.
This wanderer's song, my soul's own voice,
Rejoices in life, in every choice.

Pulse of Night

The night's deep pulse beats soft and slow,
A rhythm only hearts can know.
Each star a beat, each moon a sigh,
A dance of light across the sky.

I feel its pulse within my chest,
A call to roam, a call to rest.
The night's embrace, my heart's delight,
Guides me through its endless light.

Crimson Dawn

The crimson dawn breaks bold and bright,
Erasing shadows of the night.
Its fire ignites my weary soul,
Makes broken pieces once more whole.

I greet the dawn with open heart,
Ready to play my destined part.
In crimson hues, I find my call,
To rise, to shine, to conquer all.

VEIL OF STARS

A veil of stars drapes soft and wide,
A cosmic cloak where dreams reside.
Each twinkling light, a tale untold,
Of mysteries vast, of hearts so bold.

I wear this veil, I claim its grace,
To wander through time's endless space.
Beneath the stars, my soul takes flight,
A spark of hope in endless night.

Gentle Ruin

In gentle ruin, beauty lies,
In crumbled stones, in faded skies.
Each crack a story, each scar a song,
Of fleeting joys, of moments gone.

I walk through ruins, soft and still,
Finding peace in time's own will.
In every fall, a truth I see,
The heart endures eternally.

Sky's Embrace

The sky unfolds its wide embrace,
A boundless home, a sacred space.
Its azure arms enfold my heart,
Where dreams begin, where fears depart.

I rise to meet its endless blue,
My soul reborn, my spirit true.
In sky's embrace, I find my place,
A child of light, a child of grace.

Whispered Roots

The roots beneath the earth's soft skin,
Whisper tales of where I've been.
They hold me fast, they set me free,
A bridge between the world and me.

I listen close, their voices clear,
They speak of love, of hope, of fear.
In whispered roots, I find my ground,
A truth eternal, safe and sound.

FLEETING SPARK

A fleeting spark in twilight's glow,
Lights up the path where dreams may go.
It dances brief, yet leaves its mark,
A fleeting fire in endless dark.

I chase that spark with every breath,
Through life's sweet joy, through pain, through death.
Its fleeting light, my heart's own guide,
Leads me where truth and dreams collide.

OCEAN'S HEART

The ocean's heart beats deep and wide,
Its waves a song of time and tide.
Each crest a wish, each trough a sigh,
A mirror for the endless sky.

I stand before its boundless blue,
My soul reflected, strong and true.
The ocean's heart, my own aligns,
In waves of love, where hope entwines.

Dancing Dust

The dust dances in sunlight's beam,
A fleeting waltz, a living dream.
Each mote a world, each swirl a tale,
Of fragile hopes that never fail.

I join the dance, my heart set free,
A fleeting part of eternity.
In dancing dust, I see my place,
A spark of life, a touch of grace.

Eternal Bloom

An eternal bloom in silence grows,
Where love and time together flow.
Its petals soft, its roots so deep,
It guards the dreams we long to keep.

I tend this bloom with tender care,
Its fragrance fills the heart's own air.
In every petal, truth I see,
A love that lives eternally.

Shadow's Grace

In shadow's grace, I find my peace,
Where light and dark in silence meet.
Each shade a balm for weary eyes,
A truth that soothes, that never lies.

I walk through shadows, unafraid,
Their gentle touch, my heart has swayed.
In shadow's grace, I come alive,
Where hope and stillness both can thrive.

Light's Refrain

The light sings soft, a sweet refrain,
Of joys reborn through loss and pain.
Each ray a note, each beam a chord,
A song of life, of love restored.

I hum along, my heart in tune,
Beneath the sun, beneath the moon.
This light's refrain, my soul's own voice,
Sings of the heart's eternal choice.

Soul's Mirror

My soul's a mirror, clear and wide,
Reflecting truths I hold inside.
Each glance reveals a fleeting spark,
A light that glows within the dark.

I see my heart, my hopes, my fears,
Reflected through the passing years.
This mirror holds my truth, my core,
A light that shines forevermore.

WINDS OF FATE

The winds of fate blow soft and free,
Carrying dreams from you to me.
Each gust a chance, each breeze a call,
To rise, to love, to conquer all.

I sail these winds with heart held high,
Beneath the vast, unyielding sky.
In every gust, my soul takes flight,
To chase the stars, to greet the light.

Silent Shore

Upon the silent shore I stand,
With waves of time in open hand.
Each ripple speaks of days long past,
Of fleeting joys, of loves that last.

I walk the shore, my heart at peace,
Where time and tide find soft release.
In silence, truth begins to soar,
Upon this calm, eternal shore.

Starborn Cry

A starborn cry lights up the night,
A voice of hope, a spark of light.
It calls to hearts that wander far,
To find their place beneath the stars.

I hear its call, I feel its fire,
It lifts my soul, it takes me higher.
This starborn cry, my heart's own plea,
To live, to love, to simply be.

Earth's Whisper

The earth's soft whisper calls my name,
A gentle spark, a sacred flame.
Each leaf, each stone, each blade of grass,
Reflects a truth that time will pass.

I listen close, my heart aligned,
With earth's old soul, with life entwined.
Its whisper guides my every step,
Through joys I've sown, through tears I've wept.

Dawn's Promise

The dawn's soft promise lights the sky,
A vow that hope will never die.
Each ray a pledge, each hue a prayer,
To face the world with courage rare.

I greet the dawn with open soul,
Its light my guide, my heart made whole.
In dawn's sweet promise, I am free,
To chase the self I'm meant to be.

Twilight's Thread

A thread of twilight weaves the night,
Binding stars in gentle light.
Each strand a dream, each knot a hope,
A lifeline cast to help me cope.

I hold this thread, so frail, so strong,
It guides my heart where I belong.
In twilight's glow, my soul is led,
To peace, to love, to dreams ahead.

Heart's Horizon

My heart's horizon stretches wide,
Where dreams and distant stars reside.
Each step I take, each breath I draw,
Brings closer what my soul once saw.

I chase that line where earth meets sky,
Where hopes take wing and never die.
My heart's horizon, vast and free,
Holds all the world I long to see.

Moon's Caress

The moon's caress, so soft, so kind,
Soothes the heart and calms the mind.
Its silver touch, a gentle guide,
Reveals the truths I hold inside.

I bask in moonlight's tender glow,
Where love and dreams together flow.
This moon's caress, my heart's own friend,
Will guide my soul until the end.

Flame Within

A flame within my heart does burn,
A light no darkness can unturn.
It sparks with hope, it glows with grace,
A fire that time cannot erase.

I carry this, my soul's own light,
Through endless day, through endless night.
This flame within, my truth, my call,
Will shine until I've given all.

Skyward Glance

A skyward glance, my heart takes flight,
To chase the stars that crown the night.
Each twinkle holds a hope, a dream,
A spark of life, a radiant beam.

I lift my eyes, my soul set free,
To wander where the cosmos be.
In every glance, I find my way,
From shadowed night to endless day.

River's Truth

The river speaks a truth so clear,
Its waters sing for those who hear.
Each ripple holds a tale of grace,
Of life's eternal, flowing pace.

I kneel beside its gentle stream,
And find my truth within its gleam.
The river's truth, my heart's own guide,
Flows where my dreams and soul reside.

Echoes of Home

The echoes of home call soft and low,
Through fields where childhood's memories grow.
Each sound a thread, each note a tie,
To roots beneath the endless sky.

I hear their call, my heart returns,
To where the soul forever yearns.
In echoes of home, I find my peace,
A love that time will not release.

Starlight's Weight

The starlight bears a gentle weight,
A load of dreams, a twist of fate.
Each beam a burden, soft and bright,
That guides my heart through endless night.

I carry this, my soul's own load,
Along the starlit, winding road.
In starlight's weight, I find my truth,
A spark of hope, a spark of youth.

SILENT BLOOM

A silent bloom in darkness grows,
Where only heart and spirit know.
Its petals soft, its roots unseen,
It thrives where light has never been.

I tend this bloom with quiet care,
Its beauty fills the silent air.
In silent bloom, my soul takes root,
A truth eternal, absolute.

PATH OF DUST

The path of dust winds soft and far,
Beneath the glow of every star.
Each step a tale, each grain a song,
Of where I've been, where I belong.

I walk this path, my heart held high,
Beneath the vast, unyielding sky.
The path of dust, my soul's own way,
Leads me to light, to endless day.

Dawn's Embrace

The dawn's embrace, so warm, so near,
Dissolves the night, dissolves the fear.
Each ray a touch, each hue a call,
To rise, to love, to give my all.

I stand in dawn's soft, golden light,
My heart reborn, my soul alight.
In dawn's embrace, I find my place,
A child of hope, a child of grace.

HEART'S ECHO

My heart's own echo softly sings,
Of love, of loss, of sacred things.
Each beat a note, each pulse a rhyme,
A song that weaves through endless time.

I listen close, my soul awake,
To every choice my heart will make.
This heart's echo, my truth, my guide,
Leads where my dreams and soul reside.

9 788199 246898

Printed at Repro India Ltd.